YOU GOT TO EAT COOKBOOK

Real Life Changing Dishes Diet That Will Make You Feel Better When Cooking To Lose Weight Completely

Mary J. Hale

1

TABLE OF CONTENTS

INTRODUCTION

CHAPTER 1
APPETIZER
ANTIPASTO PLATTER WITH FRIED CALAMARI
MINI CORN DOGS WITH SHRIMP AND GRITS

CHAPTER 2
PASTA DISHES
FETTUCCINE ALFREDO WITH SEAFOOD LINGUINE
POTATO GNOCCHI WITH PESTO ABD SAUCES
SPINACH RAVIOLI WITH LASAGNA

CHAPTER 3
MAIN COURSES
VEAL MARSALA WITH BEEF BRACIOLE
CHICKEN CACCIATORE WITH FRIED RICE

CHAPTER 4
INTERNATIONAL DISHES
CUBAN SANDWICH WITH MASALA TACOS
THAI PEANUT NOODLES WITH PINA COLADA

CHAPTER 5
DESSERT
PISTACHIO SEMIFREDDO
LIMONCELLO FOR DIGESTIFS

CONCLUSION

INTRODUCTION

Selina had been feeling sick and very tired for months. Her energy levels were low, and she could barely muster up the strength to get through her day. She had tried every remedy and supplement she could think of, but nothing seemed to help.

One day, while browsing online, Selina came across a book called "You Got To Eat Cookbook." Intrigued, Selina decided to give it a try and ordered it online. When the book arrived, she eagerly dove into the recipes and nutritional advice it contained.

The cookbook emphasized the importance of eating whole, nutrient-rich foods to fuel the body and boost energy levels. Selina began incorporating the recipes into her daily meals, focusing on fresh fruits and vegetables, lean proteins, and healthy fats.

As the weeks passed, Selina noticed a remarkable difference in her health and energy levels. She no longer felt sluggish and fatigued but instead felt vibrant and alive. Her skin glowed, her mood improved, and she even shed a few pounds in the process.

Selina was amazed at the transformation she had undergone simply by changing her diet. The "You Got To Eat Cookbook" had truly been a game-changer for her health and well-being.

From that day on, Selina made it a priority to nourish her body with wholesome foods and take care of her health. She was grateful for the book that had helped her regain her vitality and was determined to continue on her journey to optimal health and wellness.

CHAPTER 1

APPETIZER

ANTIPASTO PLATTER WITH FRIED CALAMARI

Ingredients:
- One pound calamari then clean and slice into rings
- 1 cup all-purpose flour
- 1 teaspoon salt
- 1 teaspoon pepper
- 1 teaspoon garlic powder
- Vegetable oil for frying
- For the antipasto platter: assorted cured meats, cheeses, olives, roasted red peppers, artichoke hearts, and breadsticks

Instructions:
1. In a large bowl, mix together the flour, salt, pepper, and garlic powder.
2. Heat vegetable oil in a deep fryer or large skillet to 350 degrees Fahrenheit.
3. Dredge the calamari rings in the seasoned flour mixture, shaking off any excess.
4. Carefully drop the calamari rings into the hot oil and fry for 2-3 minutes or until golden brown and crispy.

5. Take away the fried calamari from the oil and place on a paper towel-lined plate to drain excess oil.

6. Arrange the fried calamari on a large platter with the assorted cured meats, cheeses, olives, roasted red peppers, artichoke hearts, and breadsticks.

7. Serve the antipasto platter with marinara sauce or aioli for dipping.

Prep Time: 20 minutes
Serves: 4-6 people

MINI CORN DOGS WITH SHRIMP AND GRITS

Ingredients:
- 1 cup cornmeal
- 1 cup flour
- 2 tsp baking powder
- 1 tsp salt
- 1 tsp garlic powder
- 1 tsp paprika
- 1 cup milk
- 1 egg
- 1 lb shrimp, peeled and deveined
- Vegetable oil, for frying
- Prepared grits

Instructions:
1. In a medium bowl, mix/stir together the cornmeal and flour and baking powder, salt and garlic powder and paprika.
2. In a different bowl, mix together the milk and egg. Pour the wet ingredients into the dry ingredients and mix/stir until well combined well enough.
3. Heat the vegetable oil in a large pot or deep fryer to 350°F.
4. Skewer each shrimp with a toothpick and dip them into the cornmeal batter, making sure they are coated evenly.

5. Fry the shrimp in batches for 2-3 minutes or until golden brown and cooked through. Take away the oil and drain on a paper towel well enough.
6. Serve the mini corn dogs with the shrimp on top of a bed of prepared grits. Enjoy!

Prep time: 20 minutes
Cook time: 15 minutes
Serves: 4

CHAPTER 2

PASTA DISHES

FETTUCCINE ALFREDO WITH SEAFOOD LINGUINE

Ingredients:
- 8 oz fettuccine pasta
- 8 oz linguine pasta
- One lb mixed seafood (shrimp, scallops)
- 1 cup heavy cream
- 1/2 cup grated Parmesan cheese
- 2 cloves garlic, minced
- 2 tbsp butter
- 1/2 tsp salt
- 1/4 tsp black pepper
- Fresh parsley, chopped (for garnish)

Instructions:
1. Cook fettuccine and linguine pasta according to package instructions until al dente. Drain and set aside.
2. In a medium skillet, melt butter over a small heat. Add garlic and sauté for one-two minutes until fragrant well enough.
3. Add the mixed seafood to the skillet and cook until fully cooked, about 5-7 minutes.

4. Pour in the heavy cream already and bring to a simmer. Stir/mix in the grated Parmesan cheese until melted well enough.

5. Add the cooked pasta to the skillet very well and toss until well coated in the sauce.

6. Season with salt and black pepper, adjusting to taste very well.

7. Serve the Fettuccine Alfredo with Seafood Linguine hot, garnished with chopped parsley.

Prep time: 30 minutes. Serves 4. Enjoy!

POTATO GNOCCHI WITH PESTO ABD SAUCES

Ingredients:
- 2 large potatoes
- 1 cup all-purpose flour
- 1 egg
- Salt and pepper to taste
- 1 cup basil pesto sauce
- Parmesan cheese for garnish
- Any additional sauce of your choice (such as marinara or alfredo)

Instructions:
1. Peel the potatoes and cut them into small cubes very well. Heat them in a pot of water until they are soft enough.
2. Mash the potatoes or pass them through a potato ricer to create a smooth texture.
3. In a large bowl, mix the mashed potatoes with the flour, egg, salt, and pepper until well combined. The dough should be soft but not sticky.
4. Divide the dough into smaller portions and roll each portion into a long rope shape on a floured surface.
5. Cut the rope into small pieces to form the gnocchi shapes.
6. Bring a medium pot of salted water to a boil and cook the gnocchi in batches until they float to the surface,

about two-three minutes. Take them away with a slotted spoon and place them on a plate.

7. In a separate pan, heat the pesto sauce over low heat.

8. Add the cooked gnocchi to the pesto sauce and toss to coat evenly.

9. Serve the gnocchi with pesto sauce topped with grated Parmesan cheese. You can also add any additional sauce of your choice on top for extra flavor.

10. Enjoy your delicious potato gnocchi with pesto and sauces!

Prep time: 45 minutes.

SPINACH RAVIOLI WITH LASAGNA

Ingredients:
- 1 package of store-bought spinach ravioli
- 2 cups of marinara sauce
- 2 cups of shredded mozzarella cheese
- 1 cup of ricotta cheese
- 1/2 cup of grated Parmesan cheese
- 1 teaspoon of dried oregano
- Salt and pepper to taste
- Fresh basil leaves for garnish

Instructions:
1. Preheat your oven to 375°F (190°C).
2. Cook the spinach ravioli according to the package instructions. Drain and set aside.
3. In a medium bowl, mix together the ricotta cheese, Parmesan cheese, oregano, salt, and pepper.
4. In a baking dish, spread a thin layer of marinara sauce on the bottom well enough.
5. Arrange a single layer of cooked spinach ravioli on top of the marinara sauce.
6. Spoon half of the ricotta cheese mixture over the ravioli and spread it evenly.
7. Sprinkle half of the mozzarella cheese on top of the ricotta mixture well enough.

8. Repeat the layering process with another layer of ravioli, ricotta mixture, and mozzarella cheese.

9. Finish with a final layer of marinara sauce and mozzarella cheese on top.

10. Cover the baking dish with aluminum foil and bake in the preheated oven for twenty-five-thirty minutes, until the cheese is melted and bubbly well enough.

11. Remove the foil and broil for an additional 5 minutes until the cheese is browned and bubbly.

12. Garnish with fresh basil leaves before serving.

13. Slice and serve the spinach ravioli lasagna hot and enjoy!

Prep time: 30 minutes.

CHAPTER 3

MAIN COURSES

VEAL MARSALA WITH BEEF BRACIOLE

Ingredients:
- 4 veal cutlets
- 4 slices of prosciutto
- 1/2 cup flour
- Salt and pepper
- 1/4 cup olive oil
- 1 cup marsala wine
- 1 cup beef broth
- 1/4 cup butter
- 1/4 cup chopped parsley
- 4 slices of beef braciole

Instructions:
1. Lay out the veal cutlets and place a slice of prosciutto on each one. Roll the veal cutlets up with the prosciutto inside and secure with toothpicks.
2. Season the flour with salt and pepper and coat the veal cutlets in the flour mixture.
3. Heat the olive oil in a medium skillet over a small-high heat.

Add the veal cutlets to the skillet and cook until browned on all sides, about 2-3 minutes per side.

4. Take away the veal cutlets from the skillet and set aside. Add the marsala wine to the skillet and deglaze the pan well enough.

5. Add the beef broth and butter to the skillet and stir until the butter is melted. Return the veal cutlets to the skillet and simmer for 5-10 minutes, until the veal is cooked through and the sauce has thickened.

6. Meanwhile, cook the beef braciole according to package instructions.

7. Serve the veal marsala with the beef braciole on top and garnish with chopped parsley.

Prep time: 30 minutes

CHICKEN CACCIATORE WITH FRIED RICE

Ingredients:
- 4 boneless, skinless chicken breasts
- 1 tablespoon olive oil
- 1 onion, chopped
- 2 cloves garlic, minced
- 1 bell pepper, sliced
- 1 cup sliced mushrooms
- 1 can diced tomatoes
- 1 teaspoon dried basil
- 1 teaspoon dried oregano
- Salt and pepper to taste
- 2 cups cooked white rice
- 2 eggs
- 1 tablespoon soy sauce
- 1 tablespoon vegetable oil

Instructions:

1. Heat olive oil in a medium skillet over a small heat. Season chicken breasts with salt and pepper very well then add them to the skillet. Cook until browned on both sides well enough, about five minutes per side. Remove chicken from skillet and set aside.

2. In the same skillet, add onion and garlic. Cook until the onion is translucent well enough, about three

minutes. Add bell pepper and mushrooms, and cook until vegetables are softened, about 5 minutes.

3. Add diced tomatoes, basil and oregano and salt and pepper to the skillet. Stir/mix to combine, then return the chicken to the skillet. Cover and simmer for twenty-twenty-five minutes, until chicken is cooked through.

4. In a separate skillet, heat vegetable oil over medium heat. Add cooked rice and soy sauce, and stir to coat. Push the rice to one side of the skillet and crack the eggs well into the other side. Scramble the eggs well enough until cooked, then mix with the rice.

5. Serve the chicken cacciatore over the fried rice and enjoy!

Prep time: 15 minutes
Cook time: 30 minutes
Total time: 45 minutes

CHAPTER 4

INTERNATIONAL DISHES

CUBAN SANDWICH WITH MASALA TACOS

Ingredients for Cuban Sandwich:
- 1 loaf Cuban bread or French bread
- 4 slices ham
- 4 slices roasted pork
- 4 slices Swiss cheese
- Pickles, sliced
- Mustard
- Butter

Ingredients for Masala Tacos:
- 1 lb ground beef or turkey
- 1 packet taco seasoning
- 8 small tortillas
- 1 cup shredded lettuce
- 1 cup diced tomatoes
- 1/2 cup chopped onion
- 1/2 cup shredded cheese
- 1/4 cup salsa
- Cilantro, chopped

Instructions for Cuban Sandwich:

1. Slice the Cuban bread in half, lengthwise.
2. Layer ham, roasted pork, Swiss cheese, and pickles on the other side of the bread.
3. Close the sandwich and spread butter on the outside of the bread.
4. Heat a panini press or skillet over medium heat. Place the sandwich on the press or skillet and cook until bread is toasted and cheese is melted.
5. Slice the sandwich diagonally and serve.

Instructions for Masala Tacos:

1. In a skillet, cook ground beef or turkey over medium heat until browned. Drain excess fat.
2. Stir/mix in taco seasoning and cook according to package instructions very well.
3. Heat tortillas in a separate skillet or microwave.
4. Assemble tacos by placing a spoonful of taco meat in each tortilla, then top with lettuce, tomatoes, onion, cheese, salsa, and cilantro.
5. Serve the Masala Tacos alongside the Cuban Sandwich for a delicious and flavorful meal.

Prep time: 20 minutes
Cook time: 20 minutes
Total time: 40 minutes

THAI PEANUT NOODLES WITH PINA COLADA

Ingredients:
- 8 oz rice noodles
- 1/4 cup creamy peanut butter
- 1/4 cup coconut milk
- 2 tbsp soy sauce
- 1 tbsp lime juice
- 1 tbsp honey
- 1 clove garlic, minced
- 1 tsp ginger, grated
- 1/2 cup pineapple chunks
- 1/4 cup shredded coconut
- 1/4 cup peanuts, chopped
- Fresh cilantro, for garnish

Instructions:
1. Cook the rice noodles according to package instructions very well. Drain and set aside.
2. In a small bowl, whisk together the peanut butter, coconut milk, soy sauce, lime juice, honey, garlic, and ginger until smooth.
3. In a medium skillet, heat the peanut butter mixture over a small heat. Add the cooked noodles and toss to coat with the sauce well enough.
4. Add the pineapple chunks and cook for another 2-3 minutes, until heated through.

5. Serve the noodles topped with shredded coconut, chopped peanuts, and fresh cilantro.
6. Enjoy your delicious Thai Peanut Noodles with Pina Colada!

Prep time: 20 minutes

CHAPTER 5

DESSERT

PISTACHIO SEMIFREDDO

Ingredients:
- 1 cup shelled pistachios
- 1 cup sugar
- 1 cup heavy cream
- 1 teaspoon vanilla extract
- 4 large eggs, separated

Instructions:
1. In a food processor, pulse the pistachios with 1/2 cup of sugar until finely ground. Set aside.
2. In a medium bowl, whip the heavy cream until soft peaks form. Stir in vanilla extract and set aside.
3. In a separate large bowl, beat the egg yolks with the remaining 1/2 cup of sugar until pale and creamy.
4. Gently fold the whipped cream into the egg yolk mixture until well combined.
5. In another clean bowl, beat the egg whites until stiff peaks form well enough.
6. Gently fold the egg whites into the cream mixture, being careful not to deflate the mixture.

7. Gently fold in the ground pistachio mixture until well distributed.

8. Pour the mixture into a loaf pan or individual serving dishes and smooth the top.

9. Freeze for at least four hours or until firm well enough.

10. Serve the pistachio semifreddo topped with extra chopped pistachios, if desired.

Prep Time: 30 minutes
Freeze Time: 4 hours

LIMONCELLO FOR DIGESTIFS

Ingredients:
- 5-6 organic lemons
- 1 liter of high-proof vodka
- 3 cups of water
- 2 cups of sugar

Instructions:
1. Use a vegetable peeler to peel the zest off of the lemons, making sure to avoid the bitter white pith.
2. Place the lemon zest strips in a glass jar and pour the vodka over them. Seal the jar and let it sit well in a cool, dark place for at least two weeks then shake the jar gently every few days.
3. After the infusion period, strain out the lemon zest from the vodka using a fine mesh strainer.
4. In a saucepan, combine the water and sugar and heat over medium heat, stirring until the sugar is completely dissolved. Let the syrup cool to room temperature.
5. Mix the sugar syrup into the lemon-infused vodka, adjusting the sweetness to your preference.
6. Pour the limoncello into glass bottles very well or jars and store them in the freezer for at least a few hours before serving.
7. Serve the chilled limoncello in small glasses as a digestive after a meal.

CONCLUSION

"You Got To Eat Cookbook" is more than just a collection of recipes - it's a culinary journey that celebrates the joy of cooking and sharing meals with loved ones. With its diverse and flavorful dishes, this cookbook serves as a reminder that food has the power to nourish our bodies and souls. Get ready to explore new flavors, create memorable meals, and make lasting connections around the dining table with the recipes in "You Got To Eat Cookbook." Happy cooking and happy eating!

Made in the USA
Columbia, SC
03 June 2025